AF342379

The Child Who Learned Dreams Come True

Written by Author
Eric Zehnder
Co - Authored by **Eugene Smith**
with **Lud Marrone**

Cover Art by
Neylan Marrone

Edited by
Eugene Smith
Cover Design by
Eugene Smith & Keith Wilke

Copyright © 2008 Eric Zehnder

All rights reserved. No part of this publication may be reproduced, stored in a retrieval system, or transmitted in any form or by any means, electronic, mechanical, photocopying, recording, or otherwise, without the prior written permission of the publisher.

ISBN: 978-1-60383-098-0

Published by:
Holy Fire Publishing
717 Old Trolley Road
Attn: Suite 6, Publishing Unit #116
Summerville, SC 29485

www.ChristianPublish.com

Printed in the United States of America and the United Kingdom

Dedication

This book is dedicated to children and the child deep within us all. That child who loves to dream, that loves to explore, that loves adventure, and that believes that great dreams can come true.

You see, we all dream dreams for reasons. Dreams are a part of our character. They encourage us, mentor to us, help us to process life and even help us through the seasons of life.

As children, we dream in our sleep and even dream dreams, while awake. We dream dreams of adventures, accomplishments, joyful times, and even of victories. We dream dreams about the future, and dreams of hope.

However there is more. This book is also dedicated to adults who have lost their desire to dream, who have lost that desire for adventure and the faith to believe that great things can and do come true.

May we all find that child deep within us all that was created to dream and may the very dreams imparted to us bring forth encouragement, excitement, creativities, wonders and new adventures to behold.

Acknowledgements

First, I must acknowledge God for the very life that I have been given, for my wonderful family, and for the promise of eternal life to come through Jesus Christ.

My precious wife Maureen, and my sons' Micah, Zachary, and Daniel who have encouraged me to live my dreams. My Father, who has mentored me and taught me many wonderful things over the course of my life. My Mother who has always been so dear to me, who is truly a gift from above. Thank you for your support, encouragement and for being the blessings that you all are.

My dear friend Lud, who has been like a brother, who has been there at so many defining moments offering love, friendship, support, and counsel.

To Neylan who provided the beautiful artwork for the cover of this book, who's friendship is like a breath of fresh air.

To Eugene and Brenda who made this book possible through persistence, perseverance, and constant encouragement at every corner.

This Book Is A Gift Especially For You:

To: ____

From: ____

Date: ____

Table Of Contents

Chapter One

A Boy Named Paul

A young boy named Paul, age 13, lived with his father and mother in a house at the foot of a central mountain of a very large mountain range in his state.

His father was a carpenter. Well, actually, we should say that he began as a carpenter, but now after many years of building he owned a company and ran a framing crew that built houses and buildings up and down the range of the mountains and small towns that were nestled against the foot of the mountains.

His mother over the years had turned their house into a wonderful home, filled with love. She brought joy and laughter to their home and the boy loved and admired his mother.

The boy's mother owned her own business, which she was able to run out of their house by the use of a computer. She was an artist and good at calligraphy. She combined the two skills to make framed plaques, with colorful art on one side, and a word of wisdom from the mountains in calligraphy on the other side. These were then put in wooden frames, and she sold them and shipped them throughout the countryside.

The boy loved the mountains and each morning when he woke up, he was eager to go outside to look at them. The mountains always greeted him and he always greeted them back with a happy and smiling heart. The mountains seemed to soar into the sky. Sometimes the boy would see a hawk or even an eagle circling high in the sky riding air currents connected to the mountain.

The boy thought that the great mountain at the foot of their home, and its two wings of ranges of mountains on each side, loved the people. They soared high, and in some ways they caused the spirits of the people to soar high also. The winds off the mountain were always fresh, and it was almost as if the mountain was glad to see you each day, as much as you were glad to see it.

The mountains were high and therefore attracted clouds and rain to themselves throughout most of the year, and lots of snow in the winter. When the mountains were covered with snow and the storm clouds had lifted, giving everyone a clear view of the mountains for miles in each direction. The boy thought they looked almost like a beautiful woman in her wedding dress. On those days, the mountain and the mountains that formed their wings, seemed to be whispering some sort of secret to the people of what people could hope for in their life and in another way, what they could attain to in life.

The rain and the melting snowfall caused a melodious river to tumble down out of the belly of the mountain until it reached the valley floor, and then headed south, paralleling the mountain range for as far as the eyes could see.

The boy had often gone to the river to play there and also to think. The boy loved the river and the sound of the river's water flowing. The boy often thought that the river was like the voice of the mountain speaking wonderful things and bringing wonderful gifts to the people.

While there, the boy often thought of the many things his father and mother had shared with him about life.

You see, he loved recalling the many special times and conversations with his father and mother, and always listened carefully to what they had to say.

As the boy was pondering, he recalled the words of his father.

Chapter Two

The Boy's Father & Mother

The boy's father had told the boy that a man or woman's thoughts, should aspire to one day being like a river. That river should be clean and constantly flowing. It should be constantly advancing and moving forward. It should never go backwards or become still. It should overcome all obstacles. It should be clear eyed, have depth, make forward movement, and be filled with beautiful, silvery things with fight in them – fish – or as his father called them, your good thoughts.

The father had said to his son, "There is a river inside of you just waiting to be tapped. Everyone has such a river – but you only come to that river by crossing a desert of making choices for the things and people that you love. You have to make choices to live, my son, and you have to be about building something. Those who do not make choices and who do not build anything will never experience the river within them."

"You see my son, deep within you is a river of creativity, vision, dreams, hope and that brings forth great things for your life and also for others. That river must be permitted to flow and be creative and never become like stagnant water."

The boy recalled that his mother had told him, "The mountain and the river are different, but they talk to each other. They bring life and beauty to each other. They give each other glory. We chose to build our house in this town, and to live by the river and the mountains. It is our hope that the river will give you its gifts. The river is ever moving, ever dynamic and ever pushing forward."

The boy also recalled that his mother had told him that the mountain will give you its gifts also. It is always solid, always making itself beautiful for you, always there for you, always giving you something higher to climb for and to achieve.

And the boy thought, "My father is like the river, in the way he runs his business, and the way he thinks about life. My mother is like the mountain, isn't she?"

Chapter Three

The Heart Of The Mountains

For many summers the father had taken the boy on horse pack trips up into the heart of the mountains. They followed the cascade trail that paralleled the tumbling, white-feathered creek, until there was a place were there was a valley in the heart of the mountains, where beaver dams backed up aqua blue pools. In these aqua blue pools, you could see both golden and rainbow trout, if you walked to the edge and peeked into the waters.

Often they would see a moose, or a bear. Once they had gotten caught between a mother moose and her calf. The mother had made movements towards them, that made them move quickly, to move out of her range into safer territory. They knew better than to stand between a mother and its young one.

The boy loved the feel of the horse beneath his saddle. His father knowing this said, "It is good for a man to feel the power of a horse and you will note my son," he said, "that a woman loves horse riding also. It is right for human beings to feel a sense of power in their lives and to have adventures with it. Just like the river deep inside of you my son, the river is also powerful and filled with adventure."

The boy and his father continued on their journey and the boy listened contently to his father's words and wisdom pondering every sentence and recalling even the words spoken by his mother, as they continued up the trail.

Chapter Four

The Campfire

Then the boy, at the evening time, when they were stopped in a meadow at a campsite, would have to help tie up the horses, after making sure they were fed. As he was doing this, his father would say to him, "Man and woman should have adventures and they also should have responsibilities. You should be able to have fun in life and with other people. But you should also be able to do something helpful and skillful with your life."

"It is important my son to have balance in your life, to enjoy your life and to enjoy others. But remember my son, to allow that river deep within you to flow and to be about moving forward in life, being creative, having vision and living out the dreams of your life"

As evening fell when all the stars had come out, as the campfire was going strong, the father would sometimes say to the boy, "And don't forget about God, my son."

He would look up at the stars and point them out to the boy, and say, "The most important lesson in life of all is to make sure that you go on living after this life. We have hearts, we have dreams, we have creativities, and we even have hopes. We were made to live a lot longer than just our thirty to ninety years. We don't know when our time will come to leave this world, my son. So let your thoughts tend towards God."

"The most important thing to settle first in your life is that your life goes on after you leave this world. Look at the darkness of the night sky," said the father, "You may only see the darkness of night, but that's not the end of the story. Then the stars come out. That's what it is like my son to live forever. We will be among those stars some day, my son. The darkness can never stop us. It just gives us our chance to shine brighter than ever."

It was on his last trip into the mountains with his father, in his thirteenth year, that the boy had experienced something special. It had happened so brightly and sprightly in his mind, that even though it happened when he was asleep, the boy could never forget it.

As the boy laid down to sleep, with thick covers over him, and a dusty makeshift pillow made out of a jacket, the boy drifted into slumber. But this time, as he moved into sleepiness, he remembered that his father and mother believed that God sometimes sent a dream to a man or a woman, or even a boy or a girl. He also remembered that the Indians had always claimed this mountain was sacred and that the spirit of God lived there. The boy thought even further as his eyes closed harder and harder, and he shifted from the realm of wakefulness into the realm of sleep, how in a way, the stars and the darkness of the sky, are kind of like interesting or bright thoughts in the darkness of the mind. The boy then saw a shooting star in his mind, cross through his mind, and then he fell asleep.

Then the boy had a dream. It was a dream of dreams and now I am going to tell you that dream - that is my purpose as a good storyteller.

Some of the dreams of men and boys, or of women and girls, come already so beautiful and so wise, that they deserve to be one of the pearls in our necklace of our fine literature and history. Our story may perhaps become part of your story.

Chapter Five

The Dream Begins

The boy himself dreamt that he was dreaming. He dreamt that he appeared before God and God was on his throne and there were angels to both the right and left side of his throne.

In the dream God leaned forward and said to the boy, "Is there something that you would like to ask of me? Is there something you wish?"

The boy, in his dream pondered for a moment, thinking as he looked around seeing all that there was to behold.

The sights, the colors, the beauty and the wonders seemed to fill his very being, as he took in all that was before him. What beauty the boy thought, what glorious beauty, as rays of light like the color of a rainbow filled his thoughts.

Then the boy answered in the dream, and said, "Yes, Lord. I would like to know how to make the fire of God."

Then God said to the boy, "This is a big request that you ask. However, it is natural to wonder about the things of God, to ponder such things and to be curious about such things. "

Then God said to the boy, "I will give you what you ask. It is a good request. But I want you to know, that when one finds the true fire of God, that fire burns forever deep within them and they will live forever. Now return to your sleep."

Chapter Six

The Woman In The Dream

Then the boy fell back into sleep and resumed dreaming in his sleep. After some time, the boy dreamt that he was walking on the narrow trail that winds up the mountain, paralleling the cascading creek. As he came around the bend, he then met a young beautiful woman. She was hiking down from the top of the mountain, towards him. As their paths crossed, they stopped and met. Then the boy said to her, "Can you help me make the fire of God?"

The woman laughed as her eyes sparkled, and she said, "I will breathe on you and give you the gift of oxygen". The boy then replied, "Yes, that would be good". He then asked the woman, "Is this important?"

Then the woman laughed again and said, "Yes, it is an important ingredient to having a great fire. I will give it to you now, as a gift from my heart." Then the woman held her hand up, palm facing the sky, and as it were, blew across that hand, a little wind into the boy. Then the two exchanged eyes and passed each other as they went their own ways.

Soon after that, the boy experienced himself in the dream, as sleeping again, and beginning to form a new dream. Slowly a new picture began to form in his mind. He saw himself walking on the earthen trail up the mountain in a place where the valley floor was flat, the trail was broader, and there was a great hillside of fallen rocks and boulders paralleling the trail.

Chapter Seven

The Old Man & The Donkey

As the boy came around the bend, he met an old man pulling a donkey and the donkey had saddlebags loaded with cords of wood draped over his back. Then the boy and the man stopped in mid-trail and greeted each other. The boy noted that although the man was old, his eyes sparkled – almost as if he was seeing a glimpse of the stars themselves in the man's eyes. Then the boy said after greeting him, "Dear sir, Can you help me build a great fire?"

The old man laughed, and said, "Of course I can and of course I will. I know how to be a friend indeed to one who is a friend in need. Let me give you some of my wood. You will need this wood in order to make a great fire."

Then the old man opened up one side of his saddlebags, and then the other, and gave the boy five good sized pieces of cut wood. The man's own axe and muscle had chopped them and now he gave them as a gift to the boy.

Then the boy said, "Thank you", and asked "is this important?"

The old man laughed, and said, "It is indeed critical if you wish to build a lasting fire."

Then the boy asked, "Is this enough to build a fire?" and the old gentleman laughed again and replied, "You need something yet to be added to your gifts. I am sure that will be coming to you soon, because God always brings things to completeness in their right time. I must go now, but I am sure something more is coming for you."

Then the boy and the old man exchanged goodbyes, and passed each other on the trail, and disappeared from one another's view.

As they disappeared from one another's view, the boy wondered what yet needed to be added to his gifts to build a great and everlasting fire.

Chapter Eight

Inspiration Point

Then the boy again experienced himself as being in the dream, falling back to sleep and starting up yet another dream.

He slept a little longer this time, but finally a dream began to form in his mind, and take on more and more substance. There he was again, walking up an even higher place on the trail that led to the top of the mountain.

He then came around the bend, to a place called Inspiration Point. Inspiration Point jetted out beyond the forest, so that from its outlook, one could see a broad panorama of the whole valley, to both the north and the south, and out to the east, and see the river winding far below, through the lush valley.

The boy noticed in the dream that it was nearing eventide, and in back of him, to the west and towards the peak of the mountain, a glorious sunset of gold, pink and purple was being painted by the hand of God in the sky, as the boy liked to think about it.

But then the boy saw a large flat boulder that jetted furthest most out into the space that surrounded the mountain, and therefore afforded the most panoramic of views.

Chapter Nine

The Young Man & His Maiden

On this flat, quite level rock, were a young man and a young beautiful maiden. They seemed to almost be a prince and a princess. They were obviously in love. They were talking to each other, back and forth, and the boy felt the love that they held for each other almost radiating from them like the brightness of the sun.

The boy noticed that the young man and his maiden genuinely loved each other, and enjoyed each other's company immensely and joyfully. He then began to cry. He did not cry the tears of sadness. Rather he cried and said to himself, "This is how I would experience love in Heaven. Heaven is real and full of love and now I am feeling the love of Heaven filling my heart. It is a great love, a love that burns like a fire and I must have this love so that I can share it with others."

The boy then closed his eyes for a minute, in the dream, there at Inspiration Point, and he saw in his mind's eye, a wonderful cloud come and hug and surround and encompass the mountain. Then a fine rain came forth. It seemed to him that he was seeing his own self, showering tears like prayers for love to come into the world, when he saw the mountain and cloud bring forth raindrops that landed on the earth.

Then the boy opened his eyes and he walked up to the young man and his princess and he said to them, "Hello. I have never met any two people so in love, who have so much warmth in their hearts. Perhaps you can help me. Can you tell me how I can build a everlasting fire?"

The young man and his maiden turned to him, and said in unison, "If we tell you how to build a fire, in the end it will be as great as that great and glorious sunset that is behind you. See how the sunset is on the one hand coming to the earth through the mountain and on the other hand drawing all men higher to itself and to new adventures. Please tell us what you already have to build your fire with?"

Then the boy said to them, "I have oxygen and breath, and I have five solid cords of hand hewn wood. Is there something more that I need?"

Then the two said to him, again in unison, "Yes, there is one more ingredient and we will faithfully give it to you." They then produced, at a point where the hand of one touched the hand of the other, each a lighted match that had been joined together at the head by the way they held them. As the boy watched their every move they said to him, "This lighted pair of matches will be necessary to create a great fire. They are already a fire in itself, but without the other ingredients, you could not have a lasting fire."

Then the boy reached out and took the matches, and said, "Thank you. But who are you, what are you? You seem more than just the average man and woman."

The man and the woman laughed, and then the man said alone, "You might say that we are kind of like what happens when the river and the mountain finally meet. We were born this way, but for man it takes a rather long journey."

Then the two appeared to rise off the earth, into the sky, and then disappear. Then the boy had the faintest notion of viewing the mountain from his home, on a clear day in the winter. It was under a sunny sky when there was one wing of white mountains to the left side of the central mountain, and one wing of white mountains to the right side, both of them stretching for miles and miles.

As the boy looked out over Inspiration Point, at the great panorama before him, he thought, "All that I can see before me is going to be mine one day. I don't know how, but in some way it will be mine. The higher I climb this mountain, which I began by following the river, now keeps on going up higher and higher. It's going into something I've never fully seen before. The more I go, the more I can see everywhere. In some way, it increases what will be mine and what more will be for those who come after me."

Then the boy, once again in his own dream, found himself sleeping. As he slept, the darkness became thicker, but it only meant that more stars came out and shined brighter and brighter.

Chapter Ten

The Dream Continues

The boy dreamt yet again. He saw himself at a place nearby the town where he lived, where the plains met the river in the town, and yet outside the town. In this spot, the plains and the river and the soaring mountains behind the river, were all in clear view.

The boy had two small pieces of bread and a fish. But he did not have a fire to cook the fish.

Then suddenly, heading towards what would be the west of him, and from the plains towards the river, then towards the mountain, three riders on grand steeds were approaching. The first horse was a paint, a mixture of white and black. The second horse was sorrel, or red. The third horse of the third rider was a golden palomino.

There was a old man riding the first horse. A young and strong man, a lot like his father, the carpenter, straddled the saddle on the second horse. A beautiful woman wearing a dress that was white and wonderful for beauty to behold was on the third horse.

She had golden hair and something that sparkled on her key finger of her right hand. It was a golden ring whose three strands united as they circled around her finger and then met in a glistening diamond joined to it at the center and top.

The old man on the first horse said to the boy, after they had come to a stop, "You haven't cooked your fish yet. Why don't you build a fire?"

The boy answering said, "I've never built a fire – at least not a lasting fire."

Then the old man said back to him, "Then you have never really been able to eat fish, have you? Why don't you try to build a fire? I think you have the ingredients now."

The boy replied back to him, "I have dreamed of building a fire – a great fire. However, I have never built a real fire before."

Then the second man on the red horse said to the boy, "I think you have what it takes to build a real fire now. Show us what you've got. Show everyone what you've got."

The boy replied to the second man on the red horse, "I don't quite know what I have. I know that I have new gifts, special gifts that were given to me by special people that I met."

Then the man on the second horse replied back to the boy, "Yes, you have been given gifts, very special gifts. But you have to use them and bring them together. When you bring them together, they are still separate gifts, but they become one very special gift"

The boy asked, "What gifts do I have?"

The old man on the first horse said to him, "What did the first person you met on the trail, the woman who laughed, who's eyes sparkled give to you?"

The boy answered, "She gave me oxygen. She breathed on me. She told me it would be a necessary ingredient to build a fire."

Then the old man on the first horse said, "Yes, oxygen is invisible, just like the heart. Oxygen is just as necessary to life as the heart and it is key to having a lasting fire. You must be sure to use that."

Then the man of the second horse said, "What did the old man with the donkey give you?"

The boy then replied, "He gave me wood, solid wood, five cords of wood that he had hand chopped himself out of a great fallen log in the forest."

Then the second rider said back to him, "You will need this solid wood to build a great fire. This wood brings body and strength to all that you do. It is a necessary ingredient for a lasting fire."

Then the woman on the golden palomino, with the golden hair, and the golden wedding band, leaned forward on her horse and said, "What did the man and woman in deep love give to you?"

The boy replied to her, "They gave to me two lighted matches, which they held together in such a way that the two heads touched each other and were both on fire."

As the woman's golden hair shined almost like the sun, she said back to the boy, "Yes, that is right. Where two spirits meet and love, there is already a fire burning."

Then the boy said to her, "But it was already a fire was it not?" and the woman replied, "Yes, you are right. For there to be fire at all, there must have always been fire somewhere to begin with. However, you could not have a lasting fire, or a great fire on earth, with just the two-lighted matches. Very often people fall in love and experience a hot flame, but it does not last. Nor does it grow to light the whole world."

Then the old man spoke up and said to the boy, "I think it is time for you to build the fire. Actually, we are very interested in seeing this."

Then the boy saw himself in the dream, put the five logs in a fire ring made out of uncut stones, and he breathed upon it, blowing a wind from the deepest part of his body, upon the wood. There were slivers of the wood that he brought, and the slivers caught fire. The fire began to grow and the wood began to glow. The fire began to grow and grow and burn brighter and brighter.

Then the boy bent over to tend the fire, he then straightened up and looked at the three riders.

Then the old man on the first horse spoke and said, "You know son, oxygen, wood, and a lighted match to begin with, they are like the heart of love, the body that serves love, and the spirit that gives fire to beauty. Really, if you are missing any one of the three parts, you cannot have a lasting fire on earth. With the match, you can have a short fire, but without all three parts, in unity, you cannot really have a lasting fire."

Then the man on the second horse spoke out and said, "As long as you keep feeding this fire, with all three ingredients and the gifts that have been given to you, the fire will never go out. It will grow and grow, and then you can light torches from it, until you have light that overcomes the darkness everywhere you go."

Then the woman rider on the third horse then said, "This fire on earth, is in its own way, like a star with a body filled with fire, come down to earth, and not only a star, but a mother of stars. Keep this fire growing and matches that burn together and the love that made you cry, will grow and grow, and nothing shall be impossible to you or mankind."

Then the boy looked closely at the golden ring on the finger on the hand of the woman. He looked then at the fire and he noted that the gold of the fire stood out to him. Then he looked back at the golden ring on the hand of the woman, and its gold was the same color as the gold of the fire. Then he said to the woman, "The gold of your ring, is like the gold of the fire, is it not?"

The woman then said, "Yes. In the end, I am, or all three of us are the reason why your fire is not only a dream."

Then the fire became bigger and bigger and brighter and brighter. Then the boy reached down, and found a rack and put the fish on it. He then put the fish and the rack into the fire. Then he began to cook it. The smell of its flavor was sweet in the air to all.

The boy then bent over to turn the fish, and did so. When he straightened up and looked out, the riders and their horses were gone.

He then looked to the west, towards the great golden sunset, and he thought he heard a neighing of horses in the wind, as he looked into the sunset.

Then the boy in his dream no longer saw himself by the fire, but saw himself simply asleep and dreaming and then he felt himself no longer dreaming just falling asleep in reality.

Chapter Eleven

The Boy Awakens

Then a strange thing happened, while the boy was actually asleep, a cold wind, as narrow as a hand, came and rubbed his face. The coolness made him wake up. He looked from beneath his covers, with his head poked out, towards a fire that was still going from when his father had built it. His father was standing up over to the side tending to the horses.

Then the boy got up and threw off his covers. There was something very sweet and wonderful in the air. He walked over to the fire. He outstretched his hands and began to warm himself and then he noticed something in the fire.

In the fire, there was a rack and on the rack there were fresh fish frying. The smell of its flavor was dream-like and irresistible.

The boy reached down and picked up a fork that lay on top of one of the racks. He used it to cut off a piece of the fish. He then brought this to his mouth. As he tasted it, he smiled, and then he looked up at the stars smiling and said. "I'm no longer just dreaming."

The End

Or is it the beginning of greater things to come… and greater things to behold…
Lets read on and find out.

A Simple Prayer

Lord, thank you for dreams. Thank you for dreams that encourage us, that bring joy and excitement to us, and that bring out such wonderful expressions of adventure, creativity, beauty and expectations of hope.

Lord, help me to dream dreams of love, dreams of joy, dreams that encourage and dreams that I can share with others, that will encourage them.

Help me Lord to be like a river flowing to others, like a fire that's love touches others and brings happiness and joy to the world.

Fill me Lord with good things, with heavenly things, with your plans and purposes for my life that I may be like a light shinning brightly, like the stars shinning before others making the world a brighter place for all to live.

Help me Lord, to be like a everlasting and great fire that burns brightly like a flame of love for all to see.

Encouraging Words That Mentor Greatness

Written By
Author, Eugene Smith

Love

Love is full of compassion, mercy, hope, forgiveness, kindness, and reaches out to others.

Love is warm, it is friendly, encourages others, builds others up, and never tears others down.

Love is like a fruit. Fruit that is sweet to the taste, that brings joy to the heart and that brings out the best in us all.

Love is a gift that we give to others, and a gift to also be received from others and held with admiration and respect.

Love is like a light that shines brightly. Love never fails, it conquers all things and overcomes all things.

Love Is The Gift Of God!

Faith

Faith is the ability to believe in great things, that great things are meant to happen to us all. That when we believe in great things, that great things will come to us, and also come to others.

Faith believes for the very best in all circumstances. It overcomes all barriers, obstacles, and hindrances. Faith has substance, purpose, and produces increased faith.

Faith presses forward, when we feel weak. Faith stands strong, when we feel that we can't, and faith brings out the best in us. Faith is hope in action. Faith is a friend to all that seek her.

Faith Comes From Heaven!

Trust

Trust is like a river flowing. It is powerful, flows richly and brings forth great things. Trust is like a seed that when sown produces wonderful friendships that last forever.

Trust is like a building block that must be honored, respected, and held with the highest of integrity.

From trust, great things are built, great friendships are formed and love is expressed. Trust brings out the best in us all and allows us all to share, to be open with others and to feel confident. Trust is honor in motion.

Trust Is Like A Key That Opens Great Doors!

Wisdom

Wisdom is the principle thing. It comes with understanding and increases our understanding. When we seek wisdom and get understanding, it is like a fine garment or a pearl of great price.

Through wisdom great things come forth, great things are forged, and greatness is achieved. Through wisdom we accomplish great things and achieve great things.

Wisdom is like a friend that helps us to achieve greatness, that empowers us to accomplish great things, and that blesses all.

Wisdom is like a fruit tree that comes forth from the application of learning. It's fruit is a blessing to us and also a blessing to others.

Wisdom Comes From God!

Friendship

Friendship is a part of the heartbeat of every person. Friends are very special to us all. They bring joy and companionship to us. They are precious like diamonds and worth far more than rubies.

Friendship is powerful and brings out the best in us and also the best in others. Friendship is like medicine to our hearts, and joy to our souls.

Friends are special and should always be treated as special. Friends are like family and should be loved, admired, honored and respected. Friendship is a very important part of each of our lives.

Friends love one another, laugh together, accomplish things together, share conversations, dream together, explore life together and they help each other in times of need. There is no end to true friendship.

You See True Friendship, Comes From God!

Encouragement

Encouragement is a gift. It is a gift to be given to others and also a gift to be received from others.

Encouragement is like a seed that when spoken produces fruit in the lives of others. Encouraging words and expressions build others up and bring out the best in them. Encouragement never tears others down or makes them sad.

We should never be like sour lemons towards others, but rather like luscious sweet fruit that is ripe, overflowing with sweetness and full of encouragement.

We should always try to encourage others in times of need and help them to overcome difficult situations. Encouragement is love and true friendship in motion.

Encouragement Is Precious Before God!

Hope

Hope is the creative part of each human being that believes for greater tomorrows. Hope is filled with brightness, expectations, faith, belief and convictions.

Hope is what great things are built from. Hope is powerful, exciting, joyful, and is like a seed that when sown, can bring fruit bearing trees forth.

Hope never fails or doubts. Hope is faith in action and believes for the best. Hope is like a beautiful sunset that shines brightly full of wonderful colors.

Hope has substance and within that substance is the ability to apply faith. Faith, that believes and hopes for greater tomorrows.

Hope Is A Gift From God To Each Of Us!

Forgiveness

Forgiveness is the ability to love others even when they have wronged you. It is the ability to look past a wrong and see something far, far greater.

Forgiveness is saying, hey we all make mistakes, but I love you more than that mistake, and you are much more important to me than the problem at hand.

Forgiveness hopes for the best in all people, even when they fall short. Forgiveness is an expression of truly loving others and a expression of compassion and mercy. Forgiveness is the application of Godly principles. Principles filled with character, compassion, mercy, and understanding. Forgiveness is all about love.

Forgiveness Is The Heartbeat Of God!

Mercy

Mercy is the ability to be merciful towards others. It is a very important part of life. You see there will be times when we need the mercy of others, that others would be merciful towards us.

Therefore, we should cloth ourselves with mercy, showing ourselves as merciful so that others will also extend mercy and compassion to us in times of need.

For we all will encounter times when we need others to have mercy on us. Therefore mercy should always triumph over judgment.

Mercy is the application of love, compassion and understanding. Mercy is a fruit of goodness and hopes for better things.

God Is A God Of Mercy!

Kindness

Kindness is the application of love towards others. It is an expression of the heart flowing with compassion.

Kindness produces wonderful things and brings joy to the hearts of others. It is love at work producing great things within us and also within others.

Kindness is love in motion, and flowing like a mighty river full of goodness, passion, and greatness.

Kindness is sweet to our ears, a blessing to our souls, and brings healing to everyone. It is overflowing with goodness, produces great character and is pleasing in the sight of God.

We should all be kind to others, making a difference in the lives of others and our world.

Kindness Is Heaven's River Flowing!

Compassion

Compassion is the ability to see beyond things. Compassion is like a river that searches things out always looking to embrace things with love.

Compassion is the fruit of love, fruit that has been watered with love, and a fruit that produces love.

Compassion is a warm fire on a cold day, a cold drink of water on a hot day and like a angel of love where hard and difficult times are found.

Compassion is like silk blowing in the wind. Compassion is soft, gentle and warms the hearts of others.

Compassion is powerful. It overcomes many things and heals broken hearts. Compassion is love and kindness in motion.

Compassion Is God's Children At Work!

Relationships

Relationships are very important. Each of us must honor our relationships with others placing others very high on our list of importance. You see we can make a difference in the lives of others.

Just imagine if each of us looked at others as more important than ourselves. Placing others before ourselves, loving others, serving others and seeking to do good to everyone we come to know. Our world would be a better place.

Sometimes relationships encounter problems and go sour. However if we choose to rise above such, we can bring healing in times of need and mend the hearts of others.

We all play an important part in relationships.

Relationships Are Dear To God!

Truth

Truth is being honest with yourself and also with others. Truth is pure, honorable, is full of integrity and is the fruit of great character.

Truth brings joy to others, it builds confidence in others and it never lies to others or tears them down.

Truth is full of light and overcomes darkness. Truth comes from a pure heart and is expressed through love.

Truth must be practiced and applied to our lives. That's because truth sets us free from lies, deceit, manipulation, deceptions, and provides the framework for greater things to come.

Truth is honesty in motion. It has purpose and is the building block of great character that is full of heavens righteousness. Great things come from truth.

Truth Is One Of God's Core Elements!

Humility

Humility is like a fine garment. When we clothe ourselves with humility, we clothe ourselves with grace and with great character.

Humility is like a beautiful garment that shines like the stars. Its brightness radiates for all to see. Humility is like a great King that humbles himself before others.

Humility is like a priceless seed that when sown produces great things, greatness and brings forth wonderful expression for others to see.

Humility is the application of being humble and through humility others see greatness deep within us. God loves when his children young and old clothe themselves with humility.

Humility is like a key that opens great doors.

God's Loves A Humble Heart!

Meekness

Meekness is precious to God. It is God's will in the lives of his children. Meekness is never prideful, it never boasts and it never seeks to rise above others.

Meekness is like humility, the application of being humble, and brings great rewards to us all. It is like a treasure chest filled with precious things.

Meekness brings forth Godly treasures and a great inheritance of greater things to come. Like as precious stones of great worth that bring joy to our lives.

God loves the meek and there are great rewards that come to those who are meek. Not only in this life but also in heaven for all eternity.

God Loves Those That Are Meek!

Generosity

Being generous is almost in a class of it's own. It defines a person's values, goodness, heart and character. Generosity is the ability to see a need and sow love into that need.

You see we all have been given gifts. Gifts to enjoy. However, those gifts are also for the benefit of others, so that we can bless others.

When we are generous to others, we extend love, compassion, kindness and through such the hearts and lives of others are healed. Our gifts are like pearls to others and like precious diamonds that touch the hearts of others.

Just imagine all the wonderful things that we each can do to be a blessing to others by being generous. Just imagine the difference each of us can make in the lives of others and our world through generosity.

God Rewards Those That Are Generous!

Giving

Giving is an expression of a heart filled with love. When we give to others, it expresses our love for others and brings expressions of love to others.

Giving is one of the many great gifts of love that is filled with compassion, friendship, kindness, and overflowing with blessings.

Giving brings joy to our hearts, great things to our lives and touches the hearts of others. It produces great character that shines for all to see.

Giving is generosity in motion. It is the application of brotherly and sisterly love towards others. It is precious in the sight of God and God rewards those who freely give to others with a humble and thankful heart.

Giving Is An Expression Of God's Love!

Joy

Joy is happiness and laughter overflowing. Sometimes it is expressed through words and expression. Other times, it is a still quietness deep within us.

Joy is like a medicine that heals, that encourages, that builds up, and that brings great things to us. For where there is joy, sadness flees. Where there is joy, depression ceases, and where there is joy, there is great freedom to be found.

Joy can be like a smooth pond, or a moving stream and can even be like a mighty rushing river. Joy is beautiful, and like a beautiful sunset for all to see.

Joy is abundantly filled with good things and brings goodness to the ears and hearts of others. It is priceless, like a picture that captures wonderful expressions.

Joy Is Our Strength & Comes From God!

Peace

Peace is like a stream that is gentle, quiet and still. Peace is like a song that brings rest to the heart and soul. Peace is soothing, relaxing and is like a soft breeze blowing across our face.

Peace is like two doves sitting quietly enjoying the simplicity of life. It is like the sun shinning after a great storm bringing forth light.

Peace is like a deep breath of fresh air or like a story that brings you to a place of rest. Peace overcomes frustrations, overcomes stress and overcomes those fearful thoughts. Peace is a friend to all who will seek her.

We should all allow peace to capture us, refresh us and flow like a mighty river from Heaven. For in peace is found gentleness, calm and quietness. Peace is fruitful and produces great fruits.

Peace Is One Of The Fruits From God's Tree!

Gentleness

Being gentle is like a soft blanket to others. It is warm, brings comfort, and filled with the expressions of love.

Gentleness is the ability to be gentle even when you are strong. It is the ability to touch others with words and expression that bring warmth to their hearts and lives.

Gentleness is filled with compassion, with kindness, with a soft heart and is like a lamp that burns brightly and brings great light to others. Gentleness produces great things, and brings forth great things.

Gentleness is being gentle and the application of being gentle. Picture a newborn baby when being held in the loving arms of his or hers mother. That gentle and soft caressing touch brings forth comfort, joy and feelings of being loved.

Gentleness is like a heart overflowing with compassion, with peace and with Heavens love. Being gentle is love and compassion in motion like a river filled with goodness.

Gentleness Is Like A Blanket From Heaven!

Self Control

Self - control is the ability to control our emotions and ponder our actions. Self - control is the ability not to react in, or around difficult situations.

Self - control is the application of applying good things over bad things and having the wisdom to make the right choices.

Self - control comes with character, builds character and must be mastered. It comes from wisdom and produces greatness, greatness of character, joy and happiness in life.

Self – control calms the storms of life, overcomes the battles placed before us and produces victory. It never surrenders to anger or bitterness. It never gives into the frustration of others or our own frustrations.

You see, self – control and the application of being in control over our own emotions helps us to make wise decisions that rise above unfortunate situations. Self – control is like a great tree that bears much fruit.

Self Control Is The Application Of Godly Principles!

Family

Family is one of the most important parts of our life. Our families are special and we are a special part of our family.

A family is like one body with many members. Each person plays an important part in that body. Each person is important.

We should all as members of our family strive to bless each other, to encourage each other, to serve each other in love and never be selfish.

You see love is the heartbeat of a family. Trust is the building block of the family. Honor is the strength of the family. Respect is the sweetness of the family and encouragement and joy is the life of the family.

Thank God for families. Thank God for our families. May we all love one another, encourage each other and bless each other.

God Created Families To Love!

Fathers

Thank God for fathers. They watch over us, care for us, mentor us, teach us and most importantly love us.

Fathers are special, by far worth more than gold, sliver or precious stones. They are full of wisdom, life's experiences and provide wise counsel.

Yet even as important as all these things are, and even greater things. Father's love us with a love that only a Father can know. They look upon us with joy, with excitement, with wonder, and with tender loving eye's that are expressions from their heart. They are gifts to us and we are gifts to them.

We should all honor our Fathers.

Father's Are Truly A Gift From God!

Mothers

Thank Heaven for Mothers. Mothers are all things to us. They are our comforters, our teachers, and our very special friends.

They care for us at every corner, and watch over us at ever intersection of life. They believe in great things for us, bring healing to our hearts, and always try to mend our daily problems.

They are like a soft wind blowing treasures into our lives. They are like a fresh spring bringing good gifts to us. They are like an angel from heaven standing by our side and encouraging us along the way.

Thank God for Mothers, for the love of a Mother and for all that our Mothers are to us.

We should always honor our Mothers.

Mothers Are Precious In The Sight Of God!

Children

Children are gifts from God. They bring joy and laughter to our world. They are tomorrow's future. Children are gifts from Heaven and are created to bring Heaven's treasures to all of us.

Children are born with Godly characters. They are humble, trusting, pure-hearted, loving, kind and filled with smiles.

We should all remain like little children, having humble hearts, being tender hearted, having trust and child like expressions that bless others.

Even as we grow, we should always allow that child deep within us to shine forth, bringing freshness, joy and expressions of beauty to others.

Children Are Precious To God!

Brothers

Not everyone has a brother. Some do and some don't. Some families consist of one child, some families consist of two sisters, and so on.

However, for those of us that do have brothers, we should honor them, love them, encourage them and speak wonderful things into their lives.

In return a brother should be filled with love, compassion, kindness, goodness and understand that he as a brother can make a wonderful difference in the life of others within the family.

You see brothers are special!

Brotherly Love Comes From God!

Sisters

Not everyone has a sister. Some do and some don't. Some families consist of one child, some families consist of two brothers, and so on.

However, for those of us that do have sisters, we should honor them, love them, encourage them and speak wonderful things into their lives.

In return a sister should be filled with love, compassion, kindness, goodness and understand that she as a sister can make a wonderful difference in the life of others within the family.

Sisters are special!

Sisterly Love Also Comes From God!

Grand Fathers

Thank God for Grandfathers. Within them is a lifetime of wisdom, knowledge and understanding about life.

They teach us great things, they share great life experiences with us, and they love us with an endless love.

Grandfathers are like roots that have been planted in great soil, that have been watered over many years by great waters, that have grown into large strong oak trees, full of wisdom.

Grandfathers are a part of the history of our families and also a part of the history of our world. Like great pioneers, that have prepared the way before us and brought great things to our world. Just imagine all the Grandfathers of time.

We should all honor our Grandfathers.

Grand Fathers Are Dear To God!

Grand Mothers

Grandmothers are very special. They are like angels in our lives, always watching over us with hearts full of love. They are special and worthy of our love.

Grandmothers are moms to our mothers. Moms filled with wisdom and experiences brought forth over many seasons of life. They are like great and wise pioneers.

Grandmothers are special and we as their grandchildren are special to them. You see we are in many ways like the fruit of their lives. Thank God for Grandmothers, for their love, compassion, wisdom and life experiences.

We should all honor our Grandmothers.

Grand Mothers Are God's Gift To Us!

The Power Of Conversation

Our words are powerful. They have the ability to encourage, build up or tear others down. We should always speak words in love, in truth and full of encouragement that build others up. We should never speak words that tear others down and cast unhappiness or judgment upon them.

You see our words are creative and have creative power within them. Power to bless others, to bring joy to the hearts of the hearer and to help others to achieve great things.

Therefore, whenever possible let our words be filled with love, encouragement, joy and hope that shines brightly into the lives of others. Seeking to make a positive difference to each and every person that we meet and cross paths with.

Our words and the words we speak are like seeds sown into the hearts of others. When those seeds are spoken and watered with love they fall into the good ground of the heart and produce sweet, luscious fruit in the lives of others.

Words of Love Are Precious in The Sight of God!

School & Education

Bright early mornings, school busses, teachers, friendships that matter, classrooms, and evening homework. School definitely comes with many things, including responsibilities.

School is one of the most important times and seasons of our lives. Through such training and wisdom is gained. Through such we prepare for the future, and school will prove to be the defining seasons of our lives in the years to come.

We should all take advantage of school, of its experience, of the friendships and especially when it comes to getting an education.

You see learning is not something we have to do. It is something that we get to do and something that will bring us joy, happiness and security in the years to come.

God Loves Seeing His Children In School!

Baby Sitting

Probably sounds like hard work, even when it comes with a reward. However it is more than merely a job that pays us money. It is a doorway of opportunity.

A opportunity to share love, joy, companionship, friendship and great times with others. It is an opportunity to be a big brother or a big sister to someone else.

You see, babysitting is more than work, more than earning some extra spending money. It is sharing your time with another person, and using that time to make a difference in their life. Babysitting is about being responsible, and using your gifts and talents in a loving and responsible way.

It is an honor to be entrusted with the responsibility to care for another human being. A honor that should be respected and held with the highest of integrity, appreciation, and humility.

God Loves Seeing His Children Serving Others!

Teaching Others

Just imagine each of us young and old. We all have the opportunities to teach and mentor others.

That younger brother or sister. Maybe someone who is struggling with their homework or other tasks.

Maybe the boy or girl next door, or even down the street. Maybe someone that is younger than us, or even a few years older.

Maybe that situation or circumstance that is difficult for someone else. You see, many times the simplicity of helping others learn can make all the difference in the world.

Is there a special gift or talent that you have learned to master, that you could bless others with?

Just think of all the opportunities that are placed before each of us, to teach and mentor others. Those questions asked of us from time to time that give us the chance to be a blessing to others by helping them.

God Is A Friend To Those Who Care About Others!

Making A Difference

Each of us can make a difference. We were created to make a difference, to make a difference in the lives of others and to bring forth rivers of good things to others.

Each of us has the power to bless others, encourage others, to mentor to others and to make a difference in the lives of all that we meet.

Just imagine all the gifts that are within each of us. We were all uniquely created. You are special and bring something special to life and the world around you.

So rise up and make a difference. Be a light that shines brightly, a pearl of great worth, a world changer that brings hope to others and that causes others to smile with joy.

God Created Us To Make A Difference!

Community

Community is the heart beat of our cities and nation. We all live in and are a part of community. Each of us can add greatness to our communities. From the smallest things to the greatest things, we all play an important role.

A community is like a body with many members. Each member has a part and role to play. Each part and role is equally important no matter how big or small.

We should all see others as important and a very important part of our community. As members of our communities we should always honor and respect others, treating others with compassion.

Just imagine if each of us set out each day to bless others within our communities. Just imagine the joy and happiness that would come forth. We can all be a part of making that happen.

God Loves A Happy Community!

Setting Goals

It is good to set goals. Having goals helps us to plan our future. We should set goals that we can achieve and accomplish, never setting goals that are too high or unreasonable.

Goals are an important part of our life. As we grow and become older our goals will change. Yet through each season of our lives and the things before us, setting goals helps us to find balance, be structured, put things into perspective and realize our limitations and abilities.

The best part is when we set our goals and set out to accomplish those goals. Just ponder for example a doctor. That doctor didn't just become a doctor over night. He or she started many years before by setting a goal and making plans to reach that goal.

It is the same with many things in life from the smallest things to the greatest things. We should all make our daily plans and also set goals for the future.

God Set Goals When He Created The Heavens & Earth!

Climbing Higher

Life will be full of mountains. Some small, some medium sized and some that are large. Regardless of the size, whenever we are faced with mountains, we should climb them and obtain victory.

Some mountains are easily climbed, while others are more difficult. However we should examine each mountain, each task or each situation before us and apply wisdom before tackling that climb.

Whenever we are faced with mountains in life that seem too difficult for us to climb. We should seek the advice of our parents, a relative or a trusted friend.

You see, when going on a climb, it's good to get advice from others who have found victory at climbing and overcoming the mountains of life.

With God's help and the help of others. We will all master the mountains that are set before us and climb to great heights.

God Created Mountains To Be Climbed!

Overcoming

Within us all is the ability to overcome situations, circumstances and obstacles. You see life can be full of them and as the years go by we will encounter many different situations.

However deep within us all, is the desire and ability to overcome, to press forward, and to find victory. Truly, we were created to be victorious.

As the years pass and as character comes forth. As we clothe ourselves with wisdom and understanding. Situation, circumstances, obstacles and all that comes with life will become easier to overcome and to gain victory over.

So never just give up or give in. Look deep inside of yourself and trust others that want to help you, and see each situation as a chance to be victorious.

God Gives Us Wisdom & Strength To Overcome!

Authority Figures

Authority figures are important. They are full of wisdom and make wise decisions. They protect us, watch over us, and help make our world a safer place.

Authority figures come in all shapes and sizes, they are found in many areas of life and are an important part of our world.

We should all respect those in positions of authority, those who have been trained, who have been educated and mastered the wisdom to make wise decisions.

From mothers and fathers, to policemen, to firemen and even the local postman. Regardless of the position or title, we should honor those with authority who use that authority to make our cities, communities and world a better place.

God Entrusts People With Authority, To Help Others!

Laying Up Treasures In Heaven

God created the Heavens. It is where God, all the angels and many people live after leaving this world. Just imagine the beauty, the wonder, and all that Heaven has to offer.

No one can earn their way to Heaven. But that's another great story to be told and learned.

However, for every good thing that we do in love, that is honorable before God. We are making deposits in our heavenly bank account.

Just imagine all the gifts and rewards that are waiting in heaven for those who lay up treasures in heaven. You see Our Heavenly Father loves to give gifts to his children.

Therefore, we should all be about doing good and be a blessing to others. For through such, we lay up treasures in heaven by being a treasure here on earth to others.

God Loves To See The Treasures Of Our Hearts!

Prayer

God created prayer so that we could share a relationship with him. Relationships are all about communication. Prayer is simply talking to God. It's that simple.

Just imagine, God who created the Heavens, the Earth, and all things hears the prayers of his children. Isn't that wonderful?

We should daily take time, and make time to pray. Simply to ask God to bless others in need or to simply ask God to help us in times of need.

You see God is Our Heavenly Father, and we can go to him during those times of need. Nothing is too hard for God. And no prayer is too small or too big for God.

After all, God created the Heavens, the Earth, and all things. Now that's pretty big.

God Loves When His Children Pray!

A Personal Note From Eric Zehnder

This is a very special gift book to give to someone you would like to encourage. You might share it with someone you love or that you feel would be encouraged and blessed by it.

I believe that the story of this book in a way is going to come true for people and things that are the stuff of great dreams are going to come their way, but they will be real!

I leave you with these last thoughts:

1) Keep faith;

2) The prepared will be rewarded;

3) If it is in your power to do good to someone, and you can chose to do so, or not to do so. Do it. It may trigger off much bigger things than you have ever imagined.

What may be given you may be so great; you can't take it in at first. But if like the innkeeper who found room for Joseph and Mary, you do your part, something wonderful may be born.

More About The Author

Eric Zehnder went to high school in Huntington Beach, Ca. He then went on to the University of California at Irvine, in Orange County, Ca. Continuing his education he went on to Graduate School at Yale University. He studied under, lived with and was the page of Yale's greatest historian. He won a President's Grant to write.

Then he came home to Huntington Beach, California, to design and build custom beach homes and participate in the family business. During the years of designing and building homes, Mr. Zehnder continued his love and passion for writing.

Mr. Zehnder has written an hour a day getting up before work for over thirty years. He kept a daily journal, connecting his writing to real-life, education and business. He has written over 200 manuscripts over the years from short stories to in depth long stories.

In August of 2006 his church called him to a 40-day prayer and fast vigil.

He traveled to Grand Teton National Park in Wyoming. There an astounding thing happened – he began writing sayings.

In the first two weeks he wrote 800 sayings. In the next two weeks he wrote 1,200 more. In the next ten days he wrote 1,000 more. In the next two days he wrote 1,000 more or a total of 4,000 sayings in 40 days.

He then went on to write 1,000 more a month. He calls this "reaching language fusion", explaining that, "Creative fusion happens when you keep getting more out than you put in." To date Mr. Zehnder's personal library of sayings consists of over 12,000 sayings.

Mr. Zehnder says, "What is going to be possible for willing people to do in reality is going to hugely increase." He says, "If you read a few, you will be entertained; but if you keep reading you'll put yourself on the path to much greater things in life."

He says, "He met the Spirit of God there in those mountains."

But on the other hand, it is of scientific note, and literary note. To give you a comparison, only three people have written 4,000 sayings in their lifetime – Solomon, Shakespeare, and Ralph Waldo Emerson.

Aren't you curious, what was written?

<u>Eric Zehnder Websites</u>

Visit our web sites and blogs, where you will find encouragement, humor, sayings, educational tools, and updates about future book releases and projects.

The Everlasting Kingdom
http://theeverlastingkingdom.blogspot.com

From The Pen Of Eric Zehnder
http://eric-zehnders-pen.blogspot.com

Sayings From The River Of God
http://sayings-from-the-river-of-god.blogspot.com

The Eric Zehnder Collection
http://the-ericzehnder-collection.blogspot.com

Future Books & Projects

We have many new book releases coming out before the years end to include, "Breaking The Code Of The Cross, The Jagged Edge Of The Cross, The River Of God" and also some books that share Eric's personal library of sayings.

For an update on new book releases, and other projects please visit our web sites and blogs where we place weekly posts for our reading audience. You may also leave us a comment, ask questions, share your thoughts, and even your interests about writing.
We look forward to hearing from you.

Thoughts On Paper

My Personal Journal

Thoughts On Paper

The following sections of this book are made available with you in mind. They are created for you to keep personal notes.

This is a great place to plan out some goals for the future, create a prayer list, and even write down some of your life dreams and hopes.

You never know, deep inside of you, you may find a desire for writing and that desire may someday become a hobby, or even a career. You may find yourself someday publishing a book and sharing great things with others.

Thoughts On Paper
Personal Notes:

Thoughts On Paper
Personal Notes:

Thoughts On Paper
Personal Notes:

Thoughts On Paper
My Prayer List

Thoughts On Paper
My Prayer List

Thoughts On Paper
My Prayer List

Thoughts On Paper
Setting Goals

Thoughts On Paper
Setting Goals

Thoughts On Paper
My Dreams

Thoughts On Paper
My Dreams

Thoughts On Paper
My Dreams

Thoughts On Paper
My Dreams

Thoughts On Paper
My Dreams

Thoughts On Paper
My Dreams

Thoughts On Paper
My Dreams

Thoughts On Paper
My Dreams

Thoughts On Paper
My Dreams